A TREASURY OF WISDOM

A Treasury of Wisdom

WRITTEN AND COMPILED
BY MARY JOSLIN

LION

Written and compiled by Mary Joslin
Illustrations copyright © 2015 Kate Forrester
This edition copyright © 2015 Lion Hudson

Published by Lion Books
an imprint of
Lion Hudson plc
Wilkinson House, Jordan Hill Road,
Oxford OX2 8DR, England
www.lionhudson.com/lion

ISBN 978 0 7459 6518 5

First edition 2015

Acknowledgments
Scripture quotations are taken or adapted from the Good News Bible © 1994 published by the Bible Societies/HarperCollins Publishers Ltd UK, Good News Bible © American Bible Society 1966, 1971, 1976, 1992. Used with permission.

Carmina Gadelica collected by Alexander Carmichael is published by Floris Books, Edinburgh.

A catalogue record for this book is available from the British Library

Printed and bound in China, November 2014, LH06

Contents

Wisdom

WISDOM MORE THAN RICHES

It is better – much better – to have wisdom
and knowledge than gold and silver.

PROVERBS 16:16

THE BENEFITS OF WISDOM

Wisdom will add years to your life.

You are the one who will profit if you have
wisdom, and if you reject it, you are the one
who will suffer.

PROVERBS 9:11–12

IN PRAISE OF WISDOM

I am Wisdom, I am better than jewels;
nothing you want can compare with me.
I am Wisdom, and I have insight;
I have knowledge and sound judgment.
To honour the Lord is to hate evil;
I hate pride and arrogance,
evil ways and false words.
I make plans and carry them out.
I have understanding, and I am strong.

I love those who love me;
whoever looks for me can find me.
I have riches and honour to give,
prosperity and success.
What you get from me is better than
  the finest gold,
better than the purest silver.
I walk the way of righteousness;
I follow the paths of justice,
giving wealth to those who love me,
filling their houses with treasures.

PROVERBS 8:11–14, 17–21

LISTEN TO THE VOICE OF WISDOM

Now, young people, listen to me.
Do as I say, and you will be happy.
Listen to what you are taught.
Be wise; do not neglect it.

Those who find me find life,
and the Lord will be pleased with them.
Those who do not find me hurt themselves;
anyone who hates me loves death.

PROVERBS 8:32–33, 35–36

WISE AND UNWISE CHOICES

Happy are those who reject the advice of evil
    people,
who do not follow the example of sinners
or join those who have no use for God.
Instead, they find joy in obeying the Law
    of the Lord,
and they study it day and night.
They are like trees that grow beside a stream,
that bear fruit at the right time,
and whose leaves do not dry up.
They succeed in everything they do.

But evil people are not like this at all;
they are like straw that the wind blows away.
Sinners will be condemned by God
and kept apart from God's own people.
The righteous are guided and protected by
    the Lord,
but the evil are on the way to their doom.

PSALM 1:1–6

WISDOM WHEN SPEAKING

Righteous people know the kind thing to say, but the wicked are always saying things that hurt.

PROVERBS 10:32

An honest answer is a sign of true friendship.

PROVERBS 24:26

Kind words bring life, but cruel words crush your spirit.

PROVERBS 15:4

THE WISDOM OF HUMILITY

If you pay attention when you are corrected, you are wise.

PROVERBS 15:31

Conceited people do not like to be corrected; they never ask for advice from those who are wiser.

PROVERBS 15:12

Arrogance causes nothing but trouble. It is wiser to ask for advice.

PROVERBS 13:10

WISDOM GIVES CONFIDENCE

Why is a clever person wise? Because he knows what to do. Why is a stupid person foolish? Because he only thinks he knows.

PROVERBS 14:8

WISE AND FOOLISH

The foolish man knows not, and knows not that he knows not.

The wise man knows not, and knows that he knows not.

CHINESE PROVERB

A SECURE FOUNDATION

Homes are built on the foundation of
wisdom and understanding. Where there
is knowledge, the rooms are furnished with
valuable, beautiful things.

PROVERBS 24:3–4

FAMILY TIES

Respect your mother and your father. Take
care of them, even when they are old and frail.
Respect them even when their mind fails.

Then in turn people will respect you, and
God will remember you kindly.

BASED ON EXODUS 20:12

THE WISDOM FROM HEAVEN ABOVE

The wisdom from above is pure first of all; it is also peaceful, gentle, and friendly; it is full of compassion and produces a harvest of good deeds; it is free from prejudice and hypocrisy. And goodness is the harvest that is produced from the seeds the peacemakers plant in peace.

JAMES 3:17–18

THE WISDOM OF SCRIPTURE

Those who travel by ship can easily find themselves blown off course. They look for some beacon or high peak that is easy to identify. Once they have found it, they can set a new course to the harbour they seek.

In the same way, Scripture guides those who are adrift on the sea of life back to the harbour of God's will.

GREGORY OF NYSSA (c.335–c.394)

THE SERENITY PRAYER

God, grant me the serenity to accept the
  things I cannot change,
The courage to change the things I can,
And the wisdom to know the difference.

ATTRIBUTED TO REINHOLD NIEBUHR (1892–1971)

WHOM TO FEAR

If someone more important than us is angry with us, we worry and fret all night, whereas we fall asleep without the slightest regret for having been disrespectful and ungrateful to God.

Now that's foolish.

JOHN OF APAMEA (FIFTH CENTURY)

WISELY SUSPICIOUS

Wisdom lies in trusting no one;
the person who is bitten by a snake
comes to fear the lizard.

JACOPONE DA TODI (C.1230–1306)

REAP THE BENEFITS

Plough in the field of wisdom; you will reap a fine harvest.

Sow the seeds of folly; you will have seven years of weeds.

ANONYMOUS

DECISIONS

Do not make important decisions at night,
when fear stalks you in the shadows.
 Wait until morning, when you can see
and think more clearly.

Anonymous

Don't make decisions when you are angry.
You will seek revenge against someone else
and end up hurting yourself.

Anonymous

MORTALITY

O God,
Teach us how short our life is,
so that we may become wise.

PSALM 90:12

THE HARSH REALITY

I realized another thing, that in this world fast
runners do not always win the race, and the
brave do not always win the battle. The wise
do not always earn a living, intelligent people
do not always get rich, and capable people
do not always rise to high positions. Bad luck
happens to everyone.

After all this, there is only one thing to
say: have reverence for God, and obey his
commands, because this is all that human
beings were created for.

ECCLESIASTES 9:11, 12:13

KNOWLEDGE AND WISDOM

Knowledge is proud that it knows so much.
Wisdom is humble that it knows no more.

WILLIAM COWPER (1731–1800)

Knowledge comes, but wisdom lingers.

ALFRED, LORD TENNYSON (1809–92)

A COSTLY EDUCATION

Experience is the best of schoolmasters, only
the school fees are heavy.

Thomas Carlyle (1795–1881)

A WARNING

Secret deeds
are unwise indeed;
deeds that are right
endure in the light.

Anonymous

WISELY AND SLOW

Wisely and slow; they stumble that run fast.

From *Romeo and Juliet*, William Shakespeare
(1564–1616)

Virtue

A CLEAR AIM

Whoever hammers a lump of iron first decides what he is going to make of it: a scythe, a sword, or an axe. In the same way we ought to make up our minds what kind of virtue we forge, or else we work in vain.

ANTHONY OF EGYPT (C.251–C.356)

A DEEP FOUNDATION

If you plan to build a high house of virtues, you must first lay deep foundations of humility.

AUGUSTINE OF HIPPO (354–430)

STARTING SMALL

If you set out to live a pure and holy life, remember you will be weak at the start and gradually become stronger. Start with small changes and leave the bigger ones till later. Don't demand perfection of yourself all at once; you are bound to fail, and then give up.

Think of people who set out on a journey. If they set out too fast, they will tire themselves and make themselves ill. Then they will waste a lot of time recovering.

If they start walking at a gentle pace, they will grow fitter and stronger. Then they will be able to walk many miles.

EVAGRIUS OF PONTUS (C.345–399)

OBEDIENCE

Obedience is the only virtue that plants the other virtues in the heart and preserves them after they have been planted.

GREGORY THE GREAT (C.540–604)

A NUISANCE ABOUT THE PLACE

If ever there was a monastery that doesn't have an awkward and ill-tempered person in the community, it would be necessary to go and find one.

Such a person is a real trial, but learning to deal with them wisely brings astonishing results.

BERNARD OF CLAIRVAUX (C.1091–1153)

THE PERILS OF AIMING HIGH

The higher the hill, the stronger the wind: so the loftier the life, the stronger the enemy's temptations.

JOHN WYCLIFFE (c.1330–84)

HUMBLE SERVICE

Jesus said:
Suppose one of you has a servant who is
ploughing or looking after the sheep. When
he comes in from the field, do you tell him
to hurry and eat his meal? Of course not!
Instead, you say to him, "Get my supper
ready, then put on your apron and wait on me
while I eat and drink; after that you may have
your meal." The servant does not deserve
thanks for obeying orders, does he? It is the
same with you; when you have done all you
have been told to do, say, "We are ordinary
servants; we have only done our duty."

LUKE 17:7–10

SAUCEPANS AND BROOMS

I find a heaven in the midst of saucepans and
brooms.

STANISLAUS KOSTKA (1550–68)

THE BENEFIT OF EXPERIENCE

To reach something good it is very useful to have gone astray, and thus acquire experience.

TERESA OF ÁVILA (1515–82)

LEARNING FROM MISTAKES

Take the very stones over which you have stumbled and fallen, and use them to pave your road to heaven.

JOSEPHINE BUTLER (1828–1906)

THE RIGHT WAY

There is no road or ready way to virtue.

THOMAS BROWNE (1605–82)

NO SHORT CUTS

Wickedness is always easier than virtue, for it takes the short cut to everything.

SAMUEL JOHNSON (1709–84)

PLODDING ALONG

I can plod. I can persevere in any definite pursuit. To this I owe everything.

William Carey (1761–1834)

SMALL BEGINNINGS

Start by doing what is necessary; then do what is possible, and suddenly you are doing the impossible.

Francis of Assisi (c.1181–1226)

DAILY TASKS

Thank God every morning when you get up that you have something to do which must be done, whether you like it or not. Being forced to work, and forced to do your best, will breed in you temperance, self-control, diligence, strength of will, content, and a hundred other virtues which the idle never know.

CHARLES KINGSLEY (1819–75)

HUMILITY

The higher your status, the more humbly you should behave.

ANONYMOUS

PRIDE

You can have no greater sign of a confirmed pride than when you think you are humble enough.

WILLIAM LAW (1686–1761)

THE PURPOSE OF LIFE

The purpose of life is not to be happy.
It is to be useful, to be honourable, to
be compassionate, to have it make some
difference that you have lived and lived well.

RALPH WALDO EMERSON (1803–82)

SELF-RESPECT

Never do anything that makes you ashamed
of yourself.

ANONYMOUS

HAPPINESS

Find joy in good deeds; then do more of what
makes you happy.

ANONYMOUS

SELF-AWARENESS

How few there are who have courage enough to own their faults, or resolution enough to mend them.

BENJAMIN FRANKLIN (1706–90)

A CONFESSION

Oh dear. I have nothing to leave you when I die except my bad example.

PAUL OF THE CROSS (1694–1775)

MY CONTRIBUTION

I am only one but I am still one. I cannot do everything but still I can do something; and because I cannot do everything let me not refuse to do the something that I can do.

EDWARD EVERETT HALE (1822–1909)

A LIFE WORTH LIVING

Command those who are rich in the things of this life not to be proud, but to place their hope, not in such an uncertain thing as riches, but in God, who generously gives us everything for our enjoyment. Command them to do good, to be rich in good works, to be generous and ready to share with others. In this way they will store up for themselves a treasure which will be a solid foundation for the future. And then they will be able to win the life which is true life.

WORDS OF PAUL TO A YOUNG CHRISTIAN LEADER,
1 TIMOTHY 6:17–19

A WARNING

Every tree that does not bear good fruit will be cut down and thrown into the fire.

WORDS OF JOHN THE BAPTIST, MATTHEW 3:10

GOD'S LAWS

Lord, you have given us your laws
And told us to obey them faithfully.
How I hope that I shall be faithful in keeping
  your instructions!
If I pay attention to all your commands,
Then I will not be put to shame.

PSALM 119:4–6

ON THE SAME SIDE AS GOD

My great concern is not whether God is on
our side; my great concern is to be on God's
side.

ABRAHAM LINCOLN (1809–65)

RIGHT AND WRONG

Right is right even if nobody does it. Wrong is wrong even if everybody is wrong about it.

G. K. CHESTERTON (1874–1936)

DARK SECRETS

Jesus said:
Whatever is covered up will be uncovered,
and every secret will be made known. So then,
whatever you have said in the dark will be
heard in broad daylight, and whatever you
have whispered in private in a closed room
will be shouted from the housetops.

LUKE 12:2–3

THE RIGHT TIME

There is never a wrong time to do the right thing.

ANONYMOUS

Riches

PEACE AND ABUNDANCE

"The days are coming," says the Lord,
"When corn will grow faster than it can be
   harvested,
And grapes will grow faster than the wine can
   be made.
The mountains will drip with sweet wine,
And the hills will flow with it.
I will bring my people back to their land.
They will rebuild their ruined cities and live
   there;
They will plant vineyards and drink the wine;
They will plant gardens and eat what they
   grow.
I will plant my people on the land I gave
   them,
And they will not be pulled up again."

AMOS 9:13–15

FAIR DEALING

Do not take advantage of anyone or rob him.

Do not hold back the wages of someone you have hired, not even for one night.

Do not cheat anyone by using false measures of length, weight, or quantity. Use honest scales, honest weights, and honest measures.

Obey all my laws and commands. I am the Lord.

LEVITICUS 19:13, 35–36, 37

A WARNING

And now, you rich people, listen to me! Weep and wail over the miseries that are coming upon you!

You have piled up riches in these last days. You have not paid any wages to those who work in your fields. Listen to their complaints! The cries of those who gather in your crops have reached the ears of God, the Lord Almighty.

JAMES 5:1, 3–4

THE PERILS OF GREED

To renounce riches is the beginning and sustaining of virtues.

Riches are the beginning of all vices, because they make us capable of carrying out even our most vicious desires.

AGAPE (FOURTH CENTURY)

THE ROOT OF EVIL

What did we bring into the world? Nothing!

What can we take out of the world? Nothing!

So then, if we have food and clothes, that should be enough for us. But those who want to get rich fall into temptation and are caught in the trap of many foolish and harmful desires, which pull them down to ruin and destruction.

For the love of money is a source of all kinds of evil.

1 TIMOTHY 6:7–10

THE LURE OF WEALTH

Even if I lived in a tiny dwelling on a rock in the ocean, surrounded by the waves and cut off from the sight and sound of everything else, I would still not be free of everyday worries, nor from the fear that the love of money might come and snatch me away.

CUTHBERT OF LINDISFARNE (SEVENTH CENTURY)

WHY PEOPLE LONG FOR WEALTH

There are three things that make a person desperate to be wealthy: desire for pleasure, ostentation, and lack of trust.

The last is more powerful than the other two.

MAXIMUS THE CONFESSOR (c.580–662)

WORRYING ABOUT MONEY

If you love money, you will never be satisfied; if you long to be rich, you will never get all you want. It is useless. The richer you are, the more mouths you must feed. All you gain is the knowledge that you are rich. Workers may or may not have enough to eat, but at least they can get a good night's sleep. The rich, however, have so much that they stay awake worrying.

ECCLESIASTES 5:10–12

A HOPELESS MAZE

Theirs is an endless road, a hopeless maze, who seek for goods before they seek for God.

BERNARD OF CLAIRVAUX (c.1091–1153)

RICHES ARE FLEETING

The rich will pass away like the flower of a wild plant.

The sun rises with its blazing heat and burns the plant: its flower falls off, and its beauty is destroyed.

In the same way the rich will be destroyed while they go about their business.

JAMES 1:10–11

PAIN, CARE, AND GRIEF

Riches are gotten with pain, kept with care, and lost with grief.

THOMAS FULLER (1608–61)

RICHES IN HEAVEN

Do not store up riches for yourselves here on earth, where moths and rust destroy, and robbers break in and steal. Instead, store up riches for yourselves in heaven, where moths and rust cannot destroy, and robbers cannot break in and steal. For your heart will always be where your riches are.

WORDS OF JESUS, MATTHEW 6:19–21

TRUST IN GOD

Do not start worrying: "Where will my food
come from? or my drink? or my clothes?"
Your Father in heaven knows that you need
all these things. Instead, be concerned above
everything else with the kingdom of God and
with what he requires of you, and he will
provide you with all these other things. So
do not worry about tomorrow; it will have
enough worries of its own. There is no need to
add to the troubles each day brings.

WORDS OF JESUS, MATTHEW 6:31, 32–34

LENDING AND GIVING

Be wary of lending and generous in giving.

ANONYMOUS

GENEROSITY

Remember that the person who sows few seeds will have a small crop; the one who sows many seeds will have a large crop. You should each give, then, as you have decided, not with regret or out of a sense of duty; for God loves the one who gives gladly.

And God is able to give you more than you need, so that you will always have all you need for yourselves and more than enough for every good cause.

2 CORINTHIANS 9:6–8

FREEDOM FROM LONGING

Poverty is having nothing, wanting nothing,
and possessing all things
in the spirit of freedom.

JACOPONE DA TODI (C.1230–1306)

CONTENTMENT

There are two ways to get enough. One is to continue to accumulate more and more.

The other is to desire less.

G. K. CHESTERTON (1874–1936)

Self-control

SELF-IMPROVEMENT

If you notice something evil in yourself, correct it; if something good, take care of it; if something beautiful, cherish it; if something sound, preserve it; if something unhealthy, heal it.

Do not weary of reading the commandments of the Lord, and you will be adequately instructed by them so as to know what to avoid and what to go after.

BERNARD OF CLAIRVAUX (c.1091–1153)

PLANTING SEEDS

You cannot tell what will sprout from a
handful of seeds.
   Nor can you tell what will grow from the
slightest act of mischief nor the smallest deed
of kindness.

ANONYMOUS

WILLING TO LEARN

He that never changed any of his opinions never corrected any of his mistakes; and he who was never wise enough to find out any mistakes in himself will not be charitable enough to excuse what he reckons mistakes in others.

BENJAMIN WHICHCOTE (1609–83)

SELF-AWARENESS

We delight in wanting to make others perfect,
but we are reluctant to correct our own faults.

Thomas à Kempis (c.1380–1471)

We feel and weigh soon enough what we
suffer from others, but how much others
suffer from us, of that we take no notice.

Thomas à Kempis (c.1380–1471)

COMPLAINING ABOUT OTHERS

Gossip is so tasty – how we love to swallow it!

PROVERBS 18:8

LESS COMPLAINING, PLEASE

Never listen to stories of other people's failings. If any one should come to you complaining of another, ask them to stop.

JOHN OF THE CROSS (1542–91)

FINDING FAULT

The business of finding fault is very easy, and that of doing better very difficult.

Francis de Sales (1567–1622)

TREAT OTHERS AS YOU WANT TO BE TREATED

Do not do to another person the things you find unpleasant.

You don't like it when people slander you? Then don't slander anyone.

You don't like it when someone denounces you without cause? Then don't denounce anyone.

You don't like it when someone hates you, harms you, or steals from you. Then don't do anything of the sort to anyone else.

The person who can keep to this rule has what is needed for salvation.

ANONYMOUS SAYINGS OF THE DESERT FATHERS AND MOTHERS (FOURTH CENTURY)

KEEPING SILENT

Those who are sure of themselves do not talk all the time. People who stay calm have real insight. After all, even a fool may be thought wise and intelligent if he stays quiet and keeps his mouth shut.

PROVERBS 17:27–28

When a fool is annoyed, he quickly lets it be known. Sensible people will ignore an insult.

PROVERBS 12:16

It is foolish to speak scornfully of others. If you are sensible, you will keep quiet.

PROVERBS 11:12

CONTROLLING ANGER

However just your words, you spoil
everything when you speak them with anger.

JOHN CHRYSOSTOM (c.347–407)

REASONS FOR ANGER

Anger is never without a reason, but seldom
with a good one.

BENJAMIN FRANKLIN (1706–90)

TACT

Silence is not always tact, and it is tact that is golden, not silence.

SAMUEL BUTLER (1612–80)

WHEN TO SPEAK

Mere silence is not wisdom, for wisdom consists in knowing when and how to speak and when and where to keep silent.

JEAN-PIERRE CAMUS (1584–1652)

A GENTLE ANSWER

A gentle answer quietens anger, but a harsh one stirs it up.

<small>Proverbs 15:1</small>

HOLDING YOUR TONGUE

Remember not only to say the right thing in the right place, but far more difficult still, to leave unsaid the wrong thing at the tempting moment.

<small>Benjamin Franklin (1706–90)</small>

LISTENING

There is a grace of kind listening, as well as a grace of kind speaking.

FREDERICK WILLIAM FABER (1814–63)

PATIENCE

Be patient in times of trouble. Keep your complaints to yourself. Wait for the right moment to speak out. That is your best chance of getting what you want.

ANONYMOUS

TIMING

A party is no time to offer your words of advice.

ANONYMOUS

DO SOMETHING

Get up, get dressed, stop being a layabout,
grasp the nettle, and do some hard work.

BERNARD OF CLAIRVAUX (c.1091–1153)

BE SELF-RELIANT

Let every tub stand on its own bottom.

JOHN BUNYAN (1628–88)

THE MIDDLE PATH

The courageous person is neither cowardly
   nor reckless;
the humble person neither arrogant nor
   servile;
the modest person neither timid nor bold.

DOROTHEUS OF GAZA (SIXTH CENTURY)

ADVICE FROM A FRUGAL SAINT

Do not trust in your own righteousness, do not worry about the past, but control your tongue and your stomach.

ANTHONY OF EGYPT (C.251–C.356)

FOOD CHOICES

Choose any food you like; but don't let any food choose you.

ANONYMOUS

GETTING DRUNK

Drinking too much makes you loud and foolish. It's stupid to get drunk.

PROVERBS 20:1

DRINK

Drink not the third glass, which thou canst
  not tame,
When once it is within thee.

GEORGE HERBERT (1593–1633)

THE FRUITS OF THE GOD'S HOLY SPIRIT

What human nature does is quite plain. It shows itself in immoral, filthy, and indecent actions.

But the Spirit produces love, joy, peace, patience, kindness, goodness, faithfulness, humility, and self-control.

And those who belong to Christ Jesus have put to death their human nature with all its passions and desires. The Spirit has given us life; he must also control our lives.

GALATIANS 5:19, 22–23, 24–25

SELF-DISCIPLINE

When you begin to practise self-discipline,
it will weigh as heavily as iron fetters.
    In time, your reputation will be as a golden
crown.

    ANONYMOUS

Life of faith

THE GREAT COMMANDMENT

Jesus said:
"Love the Lord your God with all your heart,
with all your soul, and with all your mind."
This is the greatest and the most important
commandment.

The second most important commandment
is like it: "Love your neighbour as you love
yourself."

MATTHEW 22:37–39

LIGHT FOR THE WORLD

You are like light for the whole world. A city built on a hill cannot be hidden. No one lights a lamp and puts it under a bowl; instead he puts it on the lampstand, where it gives light for everyone in the house. In the same way your light must shine before people, so that they will see the good things you do and praise your Father in heaven.

WORDS OF JESUS, MATTHEW 5:14–16

GOOD DEEDS IN SECRET

When you help a needy person, do it in such a way that even your closest friend will not know about it. Then it will be a private matter. And your Father, who sees what you do in private, will reward you.

WORDS OF JESUS, MATTHEW 6:3–4

PROMISES

Do not use any vow when you make a
promise. Do not swear by heaven, because it
is God's throne; nor by earth, because it is the
resting place for his feet; nor by Jerusalem,
because it is the city of the great King. Do not
even swear by your head, because you cannot
make a single hair white or black.

Just say "Yes" or "No" – anything else you
say comes from the Evil One.

WORDS OF JESUS, MATTHEW 5:34–37

REVENGE

You have heard that it was said, "An eye for an eye, and a tooth for a tooth." But now I tell you: do not take revenge on someone who wrongs you. If anyone slaps you on the right cheek, let him slap your left cheek too. And if someone takes you to court to sue you for your shirt, let him have your coat as well. And if one of the occupation troops forces you to carry his pack one kilometre, carry it two kilometres. When someone asks you for something, give it to him; when someone wants to borrow something, lend it to him.

WORDS OF JESUS, MATTHEW 5:38–42

LOVE YOUR ENEMIES

Love your enemies and pray for those who persecute you, so that you may become the children of your Father in heaven. For he makes his sun to shine on bad and good people alike, and gives rain to those who do good and to those who do evil. Why should God reward you if you love only the people who love you? Even the tax collectors do that! And if you speak only to your friends, have you done anything out of the ordinary? Even the pagans do that! You must be perfect – just as your Father in heaven is perfect!

WORDS OF JESUS, MATTHEW 5:44–48

THE SIGN OF GREATNESS

Jesus said:
If one of you wants to be great, he must be
the servant of the rest.

MATTHEW 20:26

THE PEOPLE OF GOD

You are the people of God; he loved you and chose you for his own. So then, you must clothe yourselves with compassion, kindness, humility, gentleness, and patience. Be tolerant with one another and forgive one another whenever any of you has a complaint against someone else. You must forgive one another just as the Lord has forgiven you.

And to all these qualities add love, which binds all things together in perfect unity.

The peace that Christ gives is to guide you in the decisions you make; for it is to this peace that God has called you together in the one body. And be thankful.

COLOSSIANS 3:12–15

GENEROUS LOVE

Remember to welcome strangers into your
homes. There were some who did that
and welcomed angels without knowing it.
Remember those who are in prison, as though
you were in prison with them. Remember
those who are suffering, as though you were
suffering as they are.

HEBREWS 13:2–3

A SERVANT OF GOD

Because of God's great mercy to us I appeal to you: offer yourselves as a living sacrifice to God, dedicated to his service and pleasing him. This is the true worship that you should offer. Do not conform yourselves to the standards of this world, but let God transform you inwardly by a complete change of your mind. Then you will be able to know the will of God – what is good and is pleasing to him and is perfect.

Do not let evil defeat you; instead, conquer evil with good.

ROMANS 12:1–2, 21

CHRISTIAN WISDOM

Your [Christian] faith does not rest on human wisdom but on God's power.

1 CORINTHIANS 2:5

GOD'S STANDARD

Live a life that measures up to the standard God set when he called you.

Be always humble, gentle, and patient. Show your love by being tolerant with one another.

EPHESIANS 4:1–2

KNOWING JESUS CHRIST

Knowing God without knowing our own
wretchedness makes for pride. Knowing our
wretchedness without knowing God makes
for despair. Knowing Jesus Christ strikes the
balance because he shows us both God and
our own wretchedness.

BLAISE PASCAL (1623–62)

NEITHER SAINT NOR SINNER

Too many Christians envy the sinners their
pleasures and the saints their joy, because they
don't have either one.

MARTIN LUTHER (1483–1546)

EVERYDAY CHRISTIANITY

Our life is love, and peace, and tenderness,
and bearing with one another, and forgiving
one another, and not laying accusations one
against another.

ISAAC PENINGTON (1616–79)

Do all the good you can
By all the means you can
In all the ways you can
In all the places you can
At all the times you can
To all the people you can
As long as ever you can.

JOHN WESLEY (1703–91)

FAITH

My brothers and sisters, what good is it for
people to say that they have faith if their
actions do not prove it? Can that faith save
them? Suppose there are brothers or sisters
who need clothes and don't have enough
to eat. What good is there in your saying to
them, "God bless you! Keep warm and eat
well!" – if you don't give them the necessities
of life? So it is with faith: if it is alone and
includes no actions, then it is dead.

JAMES 2:14–17

Faith is the root of works. A root that produces
nothing is dead.

THOMAS WILSON (1663–1755)

WAITING FOR GOD

We must wait for God, long, meekly, in the wind and wet, in the thunder and lightning, in the cold and the dark. Wait, and he will come. He never comes to those who do not wait.

FREDERICK WILLIAM FABER (1814–63)

TAKE UP YOUR CROSS

Jesus said:
Those who do not take up their cross and
follow in my steps are not fit to be my
disciples.

MATTHEW 10:38

FOLLOWERS OF JESUS

Jesus promised his disciples three things – that
they would be completely fearless, absurdly
happy, and in constant trouble.

G. K. CHESTERTON (1874–1936)

HOW TO PRAY

When you pray, go to your room, close the
door, and pray to your Father, who is unseen.
    Do not use a lot of meaningless words....
Your Father already knows what you need
before you ask him. This, then, is how you
should pray:
"Our Father in heaven:
May your holy name be honoured;
may your kingdom come;
may your will be done on earth as it is in
    heaven.
Give us today the food we need.
Forgive us the wrongs we have done,
as we forgive the wrongs that others have done
    to us.
Do not bring us to hard testing, but keep us
    safe from the Evil One."

WORDS OF JESUS, MATTHEW 6:6–13

DAILY PRAYER

Prayer should be the key of the day and the lock of the night.

GEORGE HERBERT (1593–1633)

Justice

COMPASSION

If you love the justice of Jesus Christ more
than you fear human judgment then you will
seek to do compassion. Compassion means
that if I see my friend and my enemy in equal
need, I shall help them both equally. Justice
demands that we seek and find the stranger,
the broken, the prisoner and comfort them
and offer them our help.

MECHTILD OF MAGDEBURG (C.1207–C.1282)

WHAT GOD WANTS

God says this:
Remove the chains of oppression and the yoke
of injustice, and let the oppressed go free.
Share your food with the hungry and open
your homes to the homeless poor. Give clothes
to those who have nothing to wear, and do not
refuse to help your own relatives.

Then my favour will shine on you like
the morning sun, and your wounds will be
quickly healed. I will always be with you to
save you; my presence will protect you on
every side. When you pray, I will answer you.
When you call to me, I will respond.

If you put an end to oppression, to every
gesture of contempt, and to every evil word; if
you give food to the hungry and satisfy those
who are in need, the darkness around you
will turn to the brightness of noon. And I will
always guide you and satisfy you with good
things. I will keep you strong and well. You
will be like a garden that has plenty of water,
like a spring of water that never runs dry.

ISAIAH 58:6–11

GOD'S COMMANDS

God says this:
Long ago I gave these commands to my
people: "You must see that justice is done,
and must show kindness and mercy to one
another. Do not oppress widows, orphans,
foreigners who live among you, or anyone else
in need. And do not plan ways of harming one
another."

ZECHARIAH 7:8–10

WHICH SIDE TO CHOOSE

Wherever you see persecution, there is more than a probability that truth is on the persecuted side.

HUGH LATIMER (c.1487–1555)

RIGHT AND WRONG

Right is right, even if everyone is against it; wrong is wrong, even if everyone is for it.

WILLIAM PENN (1644–1718)

ILL-GOTTEN GAINS

Doomed is the man who builds his house by
    injustice
and enlarges it by dishonesty;
who makes his countrymen work for nothing
and does not pay their wages.

JEREMIAH 22:13

A JUST GOVERNMENT

Some day there will be a king who rules with integrity and national leaders who govern with justice. Each of them will be like a shelter from the wind and a place to hide from storms. They will be like streams flowing in a desert, like the shadow of a giant rock in a barren land. Their eyes and ears will be open to the needs of the people. They will not be impatient any longer, but they will act with understanding and will say what they mean.

No one will think that a fool is honourable or say that a scoundrel is honest. A fool speaks foolishly and thinks up evil things to do. What he does and what he says are an insult to the Lord, and he never feeds the hungry or gives thirsty people anything to drink. A stupid person is evil and does evil things; he plots to ruin the poor with lies and to prevent them getting their rights. But an honourable person acts honestly and stands firm for what is right.

Isaiah 32:1–8

SETTLE YOUR DISPUTES

If someone brings a lawsuit against you and takes you to court, settle the dispute with him while there is time, before you get to court. Once you are there, he will hand you over to the judge, who will hand you over to the police, and you will be put in jail. There you will stay, I tell you, until you pay the last penny of your fine.

WORDS OF JESUS, MATTHEW 5:25–26

RESOLUTION

Let us stand fast in what is right and prepare
our souls for trial…. Let us be neither dogs
that do not bark nor silent onlookers nor paid
servants who run away before the wolf.

BONIFACE (c.675–754)

MERCY

Among the attributes of God, although they are all equal, mercy shines with even more brilliance than justice.

MIGUEL DE CERVANTES (1547–1616)

If we refuse mercy here, we shall have justice in eternity.

JEREMY TAYLOR (1613–67)

Love

LOVELIKE

We should be low and lovelike and
  lean each one to the other
And patient as pilgrims,
  for pilgrims we are all.

WILLIAM LANGLAND (C.1330–C.1386)

LOVE YOUR NEIGHBOUR

A teacher of the Law came up and tried to trap Jesus. "Teacher," he asked, "what must I do to receive eternal life?"

Jesus answered him, "What do the Scriptures say? How do you interpret them?"

The man answered, "'Love the Lord your God with all your heart, with all your soul, with all your strength, and with all your mind'; and 'Love your neighbour as you love yourself.'"

"You are right," Jesus replied; "do this and you will live."

LUKE 10:25–29

LOVE ONE ANOTHER

Jesus said, "This, then, is what I command you: love one another."

JOHN 15:17

LOVE AND KINDNESS

Love your neighbour, yet pull not down your hedge.

GEORGE HERBERT (1593–1633)

Kindness is in our power, but fondness is not.

SAMUEL JOHNSON (1709–84)

LITTLE THINGS

Great works do not always lie in our way,
but every moment we may do little ones
excellently, that is, with great love.

Francis de Sales (1567–1622)

AN ETERNAL LESSON

Life is not a holiday, but an education. And
the one eternal lesson for us all is how better
we can love.

Henry Drummond (1851–97)

THE WELL OF LOVE

Where there is no love, pour love in and you will draw love out.

John of the Cross (1542–91)

JOY AND SINGING

The soul of the person who loves God is always swimming in joy, always on holiday, and always in the mood for singing.

John of the Cross (1542–91)

THE GREATEST IS LOVE

If I have no love, I am nothing.

Love is patient and kind; it is not jealous or conceited or proud; love is not ill-mannered or selfish or irritable; love does not keep a record of wrongs; love is not happy with evil, but is happy with the truth. Love never gives up; and its faith, hope, and patience never fail. Love is eternal.

Meanwhile these three remain: faith, hope, and love; and the greatest of these is love.

1 Corinthians 13:2, 4–8, 13

LOVE IN ACTION

My children, our love should not be just words and talk, it must be true love, which shows itself in action.

We love because God first loved us. If we say we love God, but hate our brothers and sisters, we are liars. For people cannot love God, whom they have not seen, if they do not love their brothers and sisters, whom they have seen. The command that Christ has given us is this: all who love God must love their brother or sister also.

1 JOHN 3:18 AND 4:19–21

LOVING DEEDS MATTER

If I can stop one heart from breaking,
I shall not live in vain;
If I can ease one life the aching,
Or cool the pain,
Or help one fainting robin
Unto his nest again,
I shall not live in vain.

Emily Dickinson (1830–86)

KINDNESS

You cannot do a kindness too soon, for you never know how soon it will be too late.

RALPH WALDO EMERSON (1803–86)

GOOD GIFTS

A kind word is worth more than a gift.
A generous person will give both.

ANONYMOUS

LOVE'S LONG SEASON

Love made me like the hazel trees,
which blossom early
in the dark days of winter
and bear fruit slowly.

HADEWIJCH OF BRABANT (THIRTEENTH CENTURY)

Forgiveness

SELF-AWARENESS

Be aware of your strengths.
Be aware of your weaknesses.

Be aware of your kindness.
Be aware of your spitefulness.

Be aware of your tactfulness.
Be aware of your rudeness.

Be aware of your truthfulness.
Be aware of your lying.

Be aware of your forgiving.
Be aware of the many times you are forgiven.

ANONYMOUS

APPEAL FOR MERCY

Throw away thy rod,
Throw away thy wrath:
>   O my God,
Take the gentle path.

For my heart's desire
Unto thine is bent:
>   I aspire
To a full consent.

Not a word or look
I affect to own,
>   But by book,
And thy book alone.

Though I fail, I weep:
Though I halt in pace,
>   Yet I creep
To the throne of grace.

GEORGE HERBERT (1593–1633)

COME BACK TO GOD

Come back to the Lord your God.
He is kind and full of mercy;
he is patient and keeps his promise;
he is always ready to forgive and not punish.

JOEL 2:13

A BLESSING

Happy are those whose sins are forgiven,
whose wrongs are pardoned.

When I did not confess my sins,
I was worn out from crying all day long.

Then I confessed my sins to you, [Lord]
I did not conceal my wrongdoings.
I decided to confess them to you,
and you forgave all my sins.

PSALM 32:1, 3, 5

ADMIT YOUR FAULTS

Never be ashamed to admit to your own faults and failings.

ANONYMOUS

OWNING UP

Never be ashamed to own you have been in the wrong; it is but saying you are wiser today than you were yesterday.

JONATHAN SWIFT (1667–1745)

HOW TO APOLOGIZE

Never ruin an apology with an excuse.

BENJAMIN FRANKLIN (1706–90)

THE COVER-UP

Almost all our faults are more pardonable
than the methods we think up to hide them.

FRANÇOIS, DUC DE LA ROCHEFOUCAULD (1613–80)

SEEING GOOD IN OTHERS

I heard of one person that if he came to one of his friends and found the room not merely untidy but dirty, he would say to himself, "This person is blessed with such single-minded devotion toward heaven that he overlooks everyday matters and has no concern about the state of his room."

But, if he visited another person and found the room tidy and neat, he would say to himself, "This place is a reflection of the person's soul."

He never judged the one as neglectful nor the other as proud. Because of his kind disposition he saw good in everyone and they were eager to be good to him. May God give us the same disposition, never to notice the failings of others.

DOROTHEUS OF GAZA (SIXTH CENTURY)

DO NOT JUDGE

Do not judge others, so that God will not judge you, for God will judge you in the same way as you judge others, and he will apply to you the same rules as you apply to others.

WORDS OF JESUS, MATTHEW 7:1–2

ACCEPT OTHERS

Be not angry that you cannot make others as you wish them to be, since you cannot make yourself as you wish to be.

THOMAS À KEMPIS (C.1380–1471)

REVENGE

It costs more to revenge injuries than to bear them.

THOMAS WILSON (1663–1755)

SEVENTY TIMES SEVEN

Peter came up to Jesus and asked, "Lord, if my brother keeps on sinning against me, how many times do I have to forgive him? Seven times?"

"No, not seven times," answered Jesus, "but seventy times seven."

MATTHEW 18:21–22

WE ARE ALL GUILTY

If someone repents of their wrongdoing, stop criticizing them.

We are all guilty of something.

<small>ANONYMOUS</small>

THE SHEPHERD AND THE FLOCK

The shepherd who speaks ill of his flock speaks ill of himself.

<small>RAYMOND LULL (c.1232–c.1315)</small>

FREEDOM IN FORGIVENESS

Two works of mercy set a person free: forgive
and you will be forgiven, and give and you
will receive.

AUGUSTINE OF HIPPO (354–430)

THE POISONOUS GRUDGE

Pardon one another so that later on you will
not remember the injury. The remembering
of an injury is itself a wrong: it adds to our
anger, feeds our sin, and hates what is good.
It is a rusty arrow and poison for the soul.

FRANCIS OF PAOLA (1416–1507)

IMPROVE

Don't be so sure of forgiveness that you go on doing wrong.

ANONYMOUS

A NEW LIFE

You must put on the new self, which is created in God's likeness and reveals itself in the true life that is upright and holy.

Get rid of all bitterness, passion, and anger. No more shouting or insults, no more hateful feelings of any sort. Instead, be kind and tender-hearted to one another, and forgive one another, as God has forgiven you through Christ.

EPHESIANS 4:24, 31–32

GOODBYES

Always say farewell graciously; you may meet again.

Anonymous

Hope

THE WAY THINGS ARE

Difficulties are not a passing condition that we must allow to blow over like a storm so that we can set to work when calm returns. They are the normal condition.

CHARLES DE FOUCAULD (1858–1916)

KEEP GOING

Whatever difficulty you face, quietly, and with dignity, refuse to give in.

ANONYMOUS

Never give in. Never give in. Never, never, never, never – in nothing, great or small, large or petty – never give in, except to convictions of honour and good sense. Never yield to force. Never yield to the apparently overwhelming might of the enemy.

WINSTON CHURCHILL (1874–1965)

DETAILS, DETAILS

Exactness in little duties is a wonderful source of cheerfulness.

FREDERICK WILLIAM FABER (1814–63)

BEYOND YOUR HOPES

If you do not hope, you will not find out what is beyond your hopes.

CLEMENT OF ALEXANDRIA (c.150–c.215)

SAINTS AND SINNERS

Every saint has a past, and every sinner has a future.

OSCAR WILDE (1854–1900)

A JOURNEY TO THE STARS

If seeds in the black earth can turn into such beautiful roses, what might not the heart of man become in its long journey toward the stars?

G. K. CHESTERTON (1874–1936)

STARLIGHT

When it is dark enough, you can see the stars.

RALPH WALDO EMERSON (1803–82)

TRUE HAPPINESS

Happy are those who know they are
    spiritually poor;
the kingdom of heaven belongs to them!
Happy are those who mourn;
God will comfort them!
Happy are those who are humble;
they will receive what God has promised!
Happy are those whose greatest desire is to do
    what God requires;
God will satisfy them fully!
Happy are those who are merciful to others;
God will be merciful to them!
Happy are the pure in heart;
they will see God!
Happy are those who work for peace;
God will call them his children!
Happy are those who are persecuted because
    they do what God requires;
the kingdom of heaven belongs to them!

Happy are you when people insult you and persecute you and tell all kinds of evil lies against you because you are my followers. Be happy and glad, for a great reward is kept for you in heaven.

WORDS OF JESUS, MATTHEW 5:3–12

IN GOD'S PRESENCE

Whether I fly with angels, fall with dust,
Thy hands made both, and I am there:
Thy power and love, my love and trust
Make one place ev'rywhere.

GEORGE HERBERT (1593–1633)

SAFE IN GOD'S LOVE

If God is for us, who can be against us?

I am certain that nothing can separate us from his love: neither death nor life, neither angels nor other heavenly rulers or powers, neither the present nor the future, neither the world above nor the world below – there is nothing in all creation that will ever be able to separate us from the love of God which is ours through Christ Jesus our Lord.

Romans 8:31, 38–39

EACH NEW DAY

Finish each day and be done with it. You
have done what you could. Some blunders
and absurdities no doubt crept in; forget
them as soon as you can. Tomorrow is a new
day. You shall begin it serenely and with too
high a spirit to be encumbered with your old
nonsense.

RALPH WALDO EMERSON (1803–82)

Thankfulness

FOR GOD'S GREATNESS

Come, let us praise the Lord!
Let us sing for joy to God, who protects us!
Let us come before him with thanksgiving
and sing joyful songs of praise.

For the Lord is a mighty God,
a mighty king over all the gods.
He rules over the whole earth,
from the deepest caves to the highest hills.
He rules over the sea, which he made;
the land also, which he himself formed.

Come, let us bow down and worship him;
let us kneel before the Lord, our Maker!
He is our God;
we are the people he cares for,
the flock for which he provides.

PSALM 95:1–7

FOR GOD'S CREATION

O God, it is right for us to praise you.
People all over the world
and across the distant seas trust in you.
You set the mountains in place by your
strength, showing your mighty power.
You calm the roar of the seas
and the noise of the waves;
you calm the uproar of the peoples.
The whole world stands in awe
of the great things that you have done.
Your deeds bring shouts of joy
from one end of the earth to the other.

PSALM 65:1, 5–8

FOR ABUNDANT HARVESTS

O God, it is right for us to praise you.
You show your care for the land by sending
    rain;
you make it rich and fertile.
You fill the streams with water;
you provide the earth with crops.
This is how you do it:
you send abundant rain on the ploughed
    fields
and soak them with water;
you soften the soil with showers
and cause the young plants to grow.
What a rich harvest your goodness provides!
Wherever you go there is plenty.
The pastures are filled with flocks;
the hillsides are full of joy.
The fields are covered with sheep;
the valleys are full of wheat.
Everything shouts and sings for joy.

PSALM 65:1, 9–13

FOR FOOD

As to the different kinds of food, we should
take a little of everything, even sweets....
We should never pick and choose, or push
our food aside, but should thank God for
everything.

NILUS SORSKY (C.1433–1508)

THE SELKIRK GRACE

Some hae meat, and canna eat,
And some wad eat that want it;
But we hae meat, and we can eat,
And sae the Lord be thankit.

ROBERT BURNS (1759–96)

FOR EACH NEW DAY

Give thanks for each new day while you have breath to do so.

Anonymous

COUNT YOUR BLESSINGS

It is hard to count your blessings when sorrow presses so much closer.

But though unnumbered, blessings still surround you.

Anonymous

HAPPINESS IN SMALL PIECES

The happiness of life is made up of minute fractions – the little, soon-forgotten charities of a kiss or a smile, a kind look, or heartfelt compliment.

Samuel Taylor Coleridge (1772–1834)

WHY BIRDS SHOULD SING PRAISES

You owe everything to the God who made you, and it is right that you should praise him at all times and in all places.

God has given you the freedom to fly wherever you choose. God gave you strong feathers for yours wings and soft feathers on your body, to keep you warm.

God kept you and your kind safe in the ark so you did not perish in the flood.

Now you and your kind are free to fly in the clear air.

You do not have to sow seed or reap a harvest: God provides food that you can freely forage and water to drink in rivers and streams.

God has given you each a home – whether on mountain crags or in green valleys – and high trees in which you can nest.

You never have to worry about what to wear, because God has clothed you in beautiful feathers.

So be mindful of all God has done for you. Shun any ungrateful thoughts.

Make it your aim to give thanks and praise to God: at all times and in all places.

FROM THE SERMON TO THE BIRDS, FRANCIS OF ASSISI (C.1181–1226)

FOR GLIMPSES OF GOD

A few minutes ago every tree was excited,
bowing to the roaring storm, waving, swirling,
tossing their branches in glorious enthusiasm
like worship. But though to the outer ear these
trees are now silent, their songs never cease.
Every hidden cell is throbbing with music
and life, every fibre thrilling like harp strings,
while incense is ever flowing from the balsam
bells and leaves. No wonder the hills and
groves were God's first temples, and the more
they are cut down and hewn into cathedrals
and churches, the farther off and dimmer
seems the Lord himself.

JOHN MUIR (1838–1914)

WILDNESS

In God's wildness lies the hope of the world.

JOHN MUIR (1838–1914)

WILDNESS AND WET

What would the world be, once bereft
Of wet and of wildness? Let them be left,
O let them be left, wildness and wet;
Long live the weeds and the wilderness yet.

FROM *INVERSNAID*, GERARD MANLEY HOPKINS
(1844–89)

WEATHER

There is no such thing as bad weather.
All weather is good because it is God's.

TERESA OF ÁVILA (1515–82)

Let us give thanks to the God and Father of our Lord Jesus Christ! Because of his great mercy he gave us new life by raising Jesus Christ from death. This fills us with a living hope, and so we look forward to possessing the rich blessings that God keeps for his people. He keeps them for you in heaven, where they cannot decay or spoil or fade away. They are for you, who through faith are kept safe by God's power for the salvation which is ready to be revealed at the end of time.

Be glad about this, even though it may now be necessary for you to be sad for a while because of the many kinds of trials you suffer. Their purpose is to prove that your faith is genuine. Even gold, which can be destroyed, is tested by fire; and so your faith, which is much more precious than gold, must also be tested, so that it may endure. Then you will receive praise and glory and honour on the Day when Jesus Christ is revealed.

1 PETER 1:3–7

FOR GOD'S SALVATION

To him who is able to keep you from falling,
and to bring us faultless and joyful before
his glorious presence – to the only God our
Saviour, through Jesus Christ our Lord, be
glory, majesty, might, and authority, from all
ages past, and now, and for ever and ever!
Amen.

JUDE 24

Pilgrimage

WHY GO ON PILGRIMAGE?

A journey to Rome will cost a great deal of
trouble, and what will it bring you?
Unless Christ goes with you on the journey,
you will not find him there.

TRADITIONAL CELTIC

GOD'S WORD

Your word is a lamp to guide me
And a light for my path.

PSALM 119:105

GOD WILL GUIDE YOU

The Lord is compassionate, and when you cry to him for help, he will answer you. The Lord will make you go through hard times, but he himself will be there to teach you, and you will not have to search for him any more.

If you wander off the road to the right or the left, you will hear his voice behind you saying, "Here is the road. Follow it."

Isaiah 30:19–21

GOD'S HELP

I look to the mountains;
where will my help come from?
My help will come from the Lord,
who made heaven and earth.

He will not let you fall;
your protector is always awake.
The protector of Israel never dozes or sleeps.
The Lord will guard you;
he is by your side to protect you.
The sun will not hurt you during the day,
nor the moon during the night.

The Lord will protect you from all danger;
he will keep you safe.
He will protect you as you come and go
now and for ever.

PSALM 121

THE NARROW GATE

Jesus said:
Go in through the narrow gate, because the gate to hell is wide and the road that leads to it is easy, and there are many who travel it. But the gate to life is narrow and the way that leads to it is hard, and there are few people who find it.

MATTHEW 7:13–14

THE WAY, THE TRUTH, AND THE LIFE

Jesus said to his disciples, "Do not be worried and upset. Believe in God and believe also in me. There are many rooms in my Father's house, and I am going to prepare a place for you. I would not tell you this if it were not so. And after I go and prepare a place for you, I will come back and take you to myself, so that you will be where I am. You know the way that leads to the place where I am going."

Thomas said to him, "Lord, we do not know where you are going; so how can we know the way to get there?"

Jesus answered him, "I am the way, the truth, and the life; no one goes to the Father except by me."

John 14:1–6

FOLLOWERS OF THE WAY

The apostle Paul declared at his trial:
I worship the God of our ancestors by
following that Way which they say is false. But
I also believe in everything written in the Law
of Moses and the books of the prophets. I have
the same hope in God that these themselves
have, namely, that all people, both the good
and the bad, will rise from death. And so I
do my best always to have a clear conscience
before God and human beings.

Acts 24:14–16

THE DANGERS OF PILGRIMAGE

The pilgrim will encounter many demons in
the search that leads to God.

Anonymous

Then war broke out in heaven. Michael and
his angels fought against the dragon, who
fought back with his angels; but the dragon
was defeated, and he and his angels were not
allowed to stay in heaven any longer.

Revelation 12:7–8

TO BE A PILGRIM

Who would true valour see,
Let him come hither;
One here will constant be,
Come wind, come weather.
There's no discouragement
Shall make him once relent
His first avowed intent
To be a pilgrim.

Whoso beset him round
With dismal stories,
Do but themselves confound;
His strength the more is.
No lion can him fright,
He'll with a giant fight;
But he will have a right
To be a pilgrim.

Hobgoblin nor foul fiend
Can daunt his spirit;
He knows he at the end
Shall life inherit.
Then fancies fly away,
He'll fear not what men say;
He'll labour night and day
To be a pilgrim.

JOHN BUNYAN (1628–88)

TRACKLESS PLACES

Beware of going into trackless places without
a guide.

ANONYMOUS

A STARTING POINT

How can you choose the right way to go if you
don't know where you are?

ANONYMOUS

A DESTINATION

If you don't know where you are going, any
road will do.

LEWIS CARROLL (1832–98)

HOW TO WALK

Few people know how to take a walk. The qualifications are endurance, plain clothes, old shoes, an eye for nature, good humour, vast curiosity, good speech, good silence, and nothing too much.

RALPH WALDO EMERSON (1803–82)

TAKING ADVICE

Make friends with many; take advice from
few.

ANONYMOUS

WHOM TO FOLLOW

Jesus said:
When one blind man leads another, both fall
in a ditch.

MATTHEW 15:14

CAUTION

Don't be too hasty to trust a new friend.

Anonymous

IN DEEP WATER

When you're testing to see how deep water is, never use two feet.

Benjamin Franklin (1706–90)

A VOYAGE OF DISCOVERY

The real voyage of discovery consists not in seeking new landscapes but in seeing things with new eyes.

MARCEL PROUST (1871–1922)

CLIMBING MOUNTAINS

Climb the mountains and get their good tidings. Nature's peace will flow into you as sunshine flows into trees. The winds will blow their own freshness into you, and the storms their energy, while cares will drop away from you like the leaves of autumn.

JOHN MUIR (1838–1914)

BEAUTY AND BREAD

Everybody needs beauty as well as bread,
places to play in and pray in, where nature
may heal and give strength to body and soul.

JOHN MUIR (1838–1914)

A PILGRIM

A pilgrim is a wanderer whose ultimate destination is beyond the world's horizon.

ANONYMOUS

TRAVEL LIGHT

The pilgrim must travel light. A heavy load is too often set down.

ANONYMOUS

UPHILL

Does the road wind uphill all the way?
   Yes, to the very end.
Will the day's journey take the whole long
  day?
   From morn to night, my friend.

But is there for the night a resting-place?
   A roof for when the slow, dark hours begin.
May not the darkness hide it from my face?
   You cannot miss that inn.

Shall I meet other wayfarers at night?
   Those who have gone before.
Then must I knock, or call when just in sight?
   They will not keep you waiting at that
  door.

Shall I find comfort, travel-sore and weak?
   Of labour you shall find the sum.
Will there be beds for me and all who seek?
   Yes, beds for all who come.

CHRISTINA ROSSETTI (1830–94)

A PILGRIM'S BLESSING

God be with thee in every pass,
Jesus be with thee on every hill,
Spirit be with thee on every stream,
Headland and ridge and lawn;

Each sea and land, each moor and meadow,
Each lying down, each rising up,
In the trough of the waves, on the crest of the
   billows,
Each step of the journey thou goest.

TRADITIONAL CELTIC, FROM *CARMINA GADELICA*

EACH PRECIOUS MOMENT

Do not spend your days hurrying to the
future, nor your evenings sighing for the past.
   Find beauty and blessing here, and now.

ANONYMOUS

Inner peace

ANXIETY

Anxiety does not empty tomorrow of its
sorrows, but only empties today of its strength.

Charles Haddon Spurgeon (1834–92)

ACCEPT WORRY

Do not worry about being worried; but accept
worry peacefully.
 Difficult, but not impossible.

John Chapman (1865–1933)

AN UNTROUBLED CONSCIENCE

When a person is content with what their own conscience is telling them, they do not seek the spotlight of other people's praise.

BERNARD OF CLAIRVAUX (C.1091–1153)

A DAY WELL SPENT

You will always have joy in the evening if you spend the day fruitfully.

THOMAS À KEMPIS (C.1380–1471)

GARDENING

What could be more delightful than creating a shared garden in good company?

ANONYMOUS

WORLDLY DISTRACTIONS

This is the reason why those who deliberately occupy themselves with earthly business, constantly seeking worldly well-being, have not God's rest in their hearts; for the love and seek their rest in this thing which is so little and in which there is no rest, and do not know God who is almighty, all wise and all good. God wishes to be known, and it pleases him that we should rest in him; for all things which are beneath him are not sufficient for us.

JULIAN OF NORWICH (1342–c.1416)

THE BENEFITS OF PRAYER

If you pray truly, you will feel calm and strong,
and the angels will be your companions.

EVAGRIUS OF PONTUS (c.345–399)

INNER CONFIDENCE

If I prayed to God that everyone would
approve the things I do, I'd find myself
begging forgiveness from them all.

As it is, I pray that I may treat everyone
with the same integrity.

SARAH, DESERT MOTHER (FOURTH CENTURY)

THE PERILS OF FRETFULNESS

Scrupulous people, forever tormented by doubts and anxiety, have hearts which are not well-prepared to receive Jesus Christ. Instead of that peace which religion is meant to give, these people make their lives miserable, and full of trouble and temptation. Scrupulous people distress themselves in many ways; in fact they believe no one, and no advice brings calm to their troubled spirits. They keep going back to their sins and doubts, and the more they brood over them, the more troubled they become.

HENRY SUSO (c.1295–1366)

EVERYTHING HAS AN END

Keep your heart in peace; let nothing in this
world disturb it: everything has an end.

JOHN OF THE CROSS (1542–91)

ALL THINGS ARE PASSING

Let nothing disturb you,
Nothing frighten you;
All things are passing;
God never changes;
Patient endurance
Attains all things;
Whoever possesses God
Lacks nothing;
God alone suffices.

TERESA OF ÁVILA (1515–82)

THE PEACE OF GOD

Don't worry about anything, but in all your prayers ask God for what you need, always asking him with a thankful heart.

And God's peace, which is far beyond human understanding, will keep your hearts and minds safe in union with Christ Jesus.

Fill your minds with those things that are good and that deserve praise: things that are true, noble, right, pure, lovely, and honourable.

PHILIPPIANS 4:6–7, 8

IN GOD'S ARMS

Lord, I have given up my pride
and turned away from my arrogance.
I am not concerned with great matters
or with subjects too difficult for me.
Instead, I am content and at peace.
As a child lies quietly in its mother's arms,
so my heart is quiet within me.

PSALM 131:1–2

GOD'S FAITHFULNESS

Hope returns when I remember this one
thing:

The Lord's unfailing love and mercy still
  continue,
Fresh as the morning, as sure as the sunrise.

LAMENTATIONS 3:21–23

THE GOOD SHEPHERD

God says this:
I myself will look for my sheep and take care of them in the same way as shepherds take care of their sheep that were scattered and are brought together again.

I will let them graze in safety in the mountain meadows and the valleys and in all the green pastures.

I myself will be the shepherd of my sheep, and I will find them a place to rest.

I will look for those that are lost, bring back those that wander off, bandage those that are hurt, and heal those that are sick.

EZEKIEL 34:11, 12, 14, 15, 16

TRUST IN GOD'S STRENGTH

Don't you know? Haven't you heard?
The Lord is the everlasting God;
he created all the world.
He never grows tired or weary.
No one understands his thoughts.
He strengthens those who are weak and tired.
Even those who are young grow weak;
young people can fall exhausted.
But those who trust in the Lord for help
will find their strength renewed.
They will rise on wings like eagles;
they will run and not get weary;
they will walk and not grow weak.

ISAIAH 40:28–31

HEAVEN-HAVEN

I have desired to go
Where springs not fail,
To fields where flies no sharp and sided hail
And a few lilies blow.

And I have asked to be
Where no storms come,
Where the green swell is in the havens dumb,
And out of the swing of the sea.

GERARD MANLEY HOPKINS (1844–89)

WORDS OF JESUS

Jesus said: '
Peace is what I leave with you; it is my own
peace that I give you. I do not give it as the
world does. Do not be worried and upset;
do not be afraid.

JOHN 14:27

WORDS OF AN ANGEL

The angel said, "God loves you, so don't let
anything worry you or frighten you."

DANIEL 10:19

MOURNING

It is right to grieve, but do not allow grief to
rule your life.

ANONYMOUS

PATIENCE IN DESOLATION

In a time of desolation, never forsake the good resolutions you made in better times. Strive to remain patient – a virtue contrary to the troubles that harass you – and remember that you will be consoled.

IGNATIUS OF LOYOLA (1491–1556)

AN EASY YOKE

Jesus said:
Come to me, all of you who are tired from
carrying heavy loads, and I will give you rest.
Take my yoke and put it on you, and learn
from me, because I am gentle and humble in
spirit; and you will find rest. For the yoke I
will give you is easy, and the load I will put
on you is light.

MATTHEW 11:28–30

THE SIMPLEST ADVICE

Be solitary, be silent, and be at peace.

ARSENIUS (c.354–c.445)

INDEX OF FIRST LINES

Jesus said, "This, then, is what I command you: love one another" 127

Jesus said: Those who do not take up their cross and follow in my steps are not fit to be my disciples 108

Jesus said to his disciples, "Do not be worried and upset" 184

Jesus said: Whatever is covered up will be uncovered 53

Jesus said: When one blind man leads another, both fall in a ditch 190

Keep your heart in peace 206

Kind words bring life, but cruel words crush your spirit 20

Kindness is in our power, but fondness is not 128

Knowing God without knowing our own wretchedness makes for pride 104

Knowledge comes, but wisdom lingers 32

Knowledge is proud that it knows so much 32

Let every tub stand on its own bottom 85

Let nothing disturb you 206

Let us give thanks to the God and Father of our Lord Jesus Christ! 174

Let us stand fast in what is right 121

Life is not a holiday, but an education 129

Live a life that measures up to the standard God set when he called you 103

Lord, I have given up my pride and turned away from my arrogance 208

Lord, you have given us your laws 51

Love made me like the hazel trees 136

Love your enemies and pray for those who persecute you 98

Love your neighbour, yet pull not down your hedge 128

Make friends with many; take advice from few 190

Mere silence is not wisdom 82

My brothers and sisters, what good is it for people to say that they have faith if their actions do not prove it? 106

My children, our love should not be just words and talk 132

My great concern is not whether God is on our side 51

Never be ashamed to admit to your own faults and failings 143

Never be ashamed to own you have been in the wrong 143

Never do anything that makes you ashamed of yourself 47